SCHOLASTIC

Let's Find Out

My REBUS Reader

I0890046

Polar Animals Stick Together

by Pamela Chanko

SCHOLASTIC INC.

New York Toronto London Auckland Sydney New Delhi Hong Kong

Penguins do not mind cold weather.

A group of baby penguins is called a crèche.

They keep warm. They stick together!

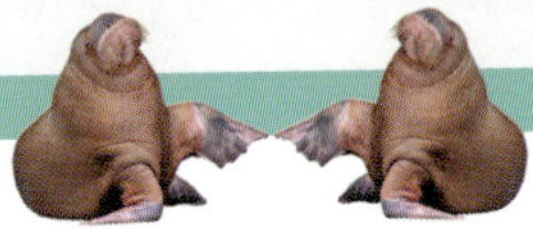

Walruses do not mind cold weather.

A group of walruses is called a pod.

They keep warm. They stick together!

Musk oxen do not mind cold weather.

They keep warm. They stick together!

What would you do in such cold weather?
It might be better to stick together!